This book belongs to

A J Marques

This book is dedicated to my children - Mikey, Kobe, and Jojo.

Ninja Life Hacks™

Funny Ninja

By Mary Nhin

Pictures by
Jelena Stupar

"All right. All right. I will guys," said Funny Ninja.

Telling jokes is easy once you understand the different types and practice them.

I like to tell three different types of jokes:

Questions-and-Answers
Knock-knocks
Riddles

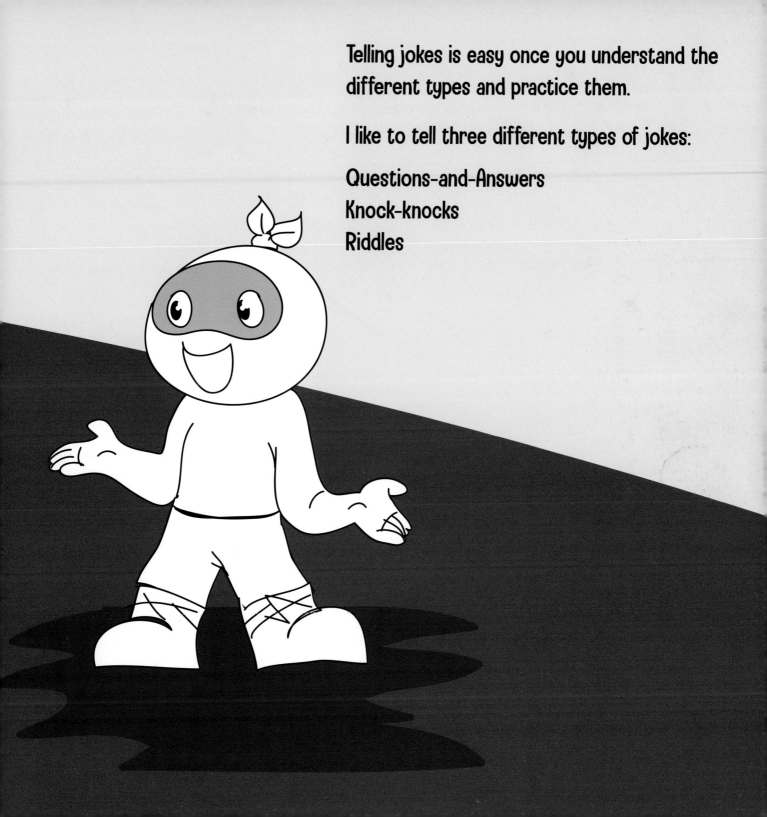

Knock-knock jokes are the easiest to remember. Here are some:

Knock, knock

Who's there?

Alaska.

Alaska who?

Alaska Santa for a new bike.

Knock, knock

Who's there?

Chick.

Chick who?

Chick your shoelaces. They're untied.

Knock, knock

Who's there?

Mary.

Mary who?

Mary Christmas.

Knock, knock

Who's there?

Radio.

Radio who?

Radio or not, here I come.

Knock, knock

Who's there?

Barbie.

Barbie who?

Barbie Q. Chicken.

Knock, knock

Who's there?

Monkey.

Monkey who?

Monkey see.
Monkey do.

Knock, knock

Who's there?

Doughnut.

Doughnut who?

Doughnut ask where the treasure is. It's a secret.

Knock, knock

Who's there?

Sir.

Sir who?

Surprise. I have a gift for you.

Knock, knock

Who's there?

Ice cream.

Ice cream who?

**Ice cream
with happiness!**

Knock, knock

Who's there?

Owls.

Owls who?

Why, yes, they do.

Knock, knock

Who's there?

Phillip.

Phillip who?

Please Phillip my bag with candy.

Knock, knock

Who's there?

Pecan.

Pecan who?

Pecan somebody your own size.

Then, there are riddles. Riddles are word puzzles that are funny!
Here are some:

And that's all there is to it!
Now, it's your turn.

Please visit us at ninjalifehacks.tv to check out our box sets!

Knock, knock

Who's there?

I love.

I love who?

I don't know, you tell me!

Knock, knock

Who's there?

Nun.

Nun who?

Nun of your business!

Knock, knock

Who's there?

Boo.

Boo who?

I didn't mean to make you cry! It's just me!

Knock, knock

Who's there?

Bless.

Bless who?

I didn't sneeze!

Knock, knock

Who's there?

Ketchup.

Ketchup who?

Ketchup with me and I'll tell you!

Knock, knock

Who's there?

Europe.

Europe who?

No, you're a poo!

HA HA HA